KT-872-699

ANIMAL
OPPOSITES

QED Publishing

BIG

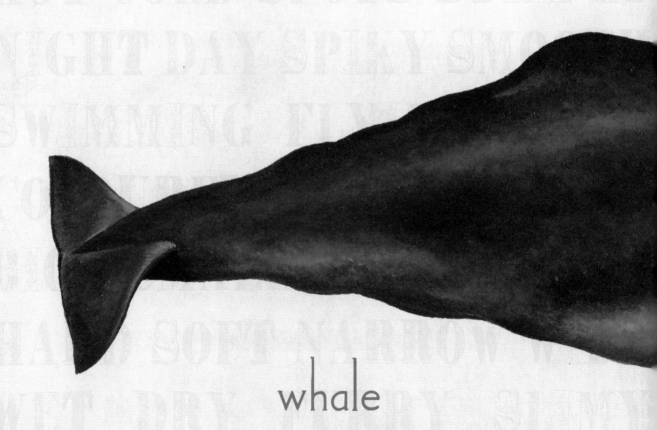

whale

SMALL

flea

bug

mouse

shrimp

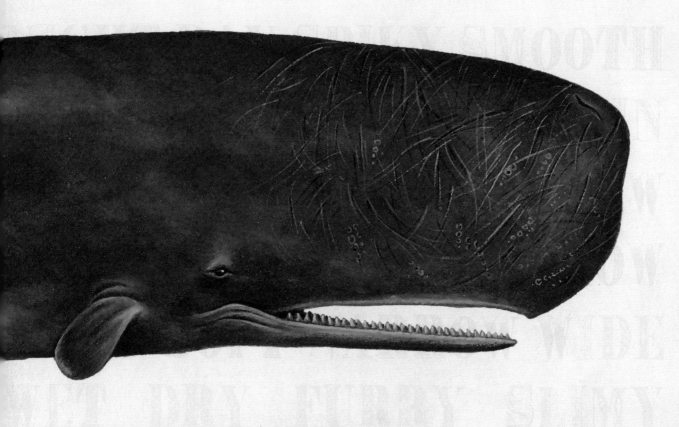

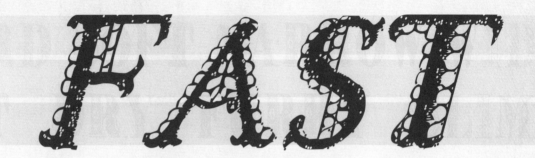

FAST

sloth

cheetah

SLOW

tortoise

snails

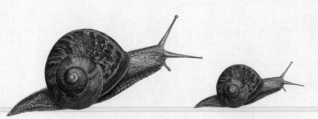

HARD

turtle

pangolin

armadillo

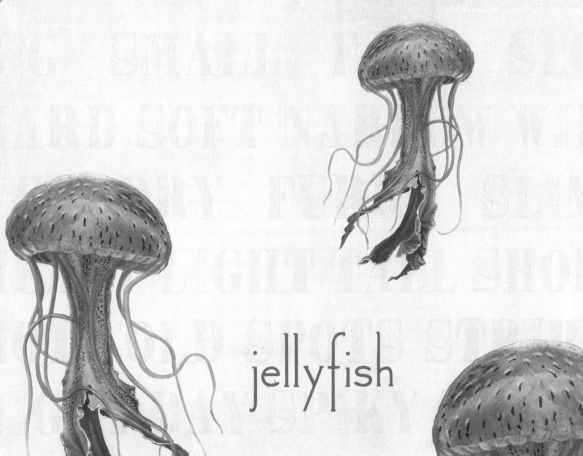

jellyfish

SOFT

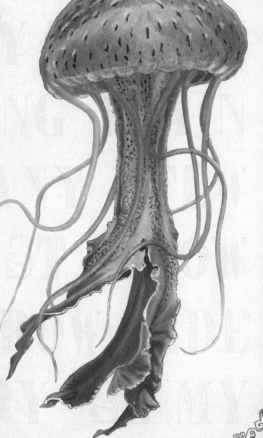

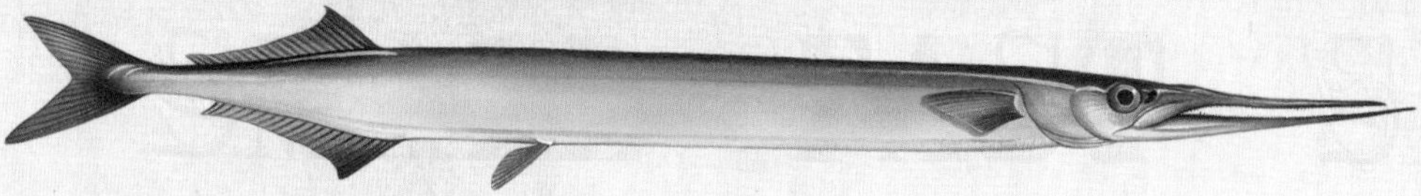

fish

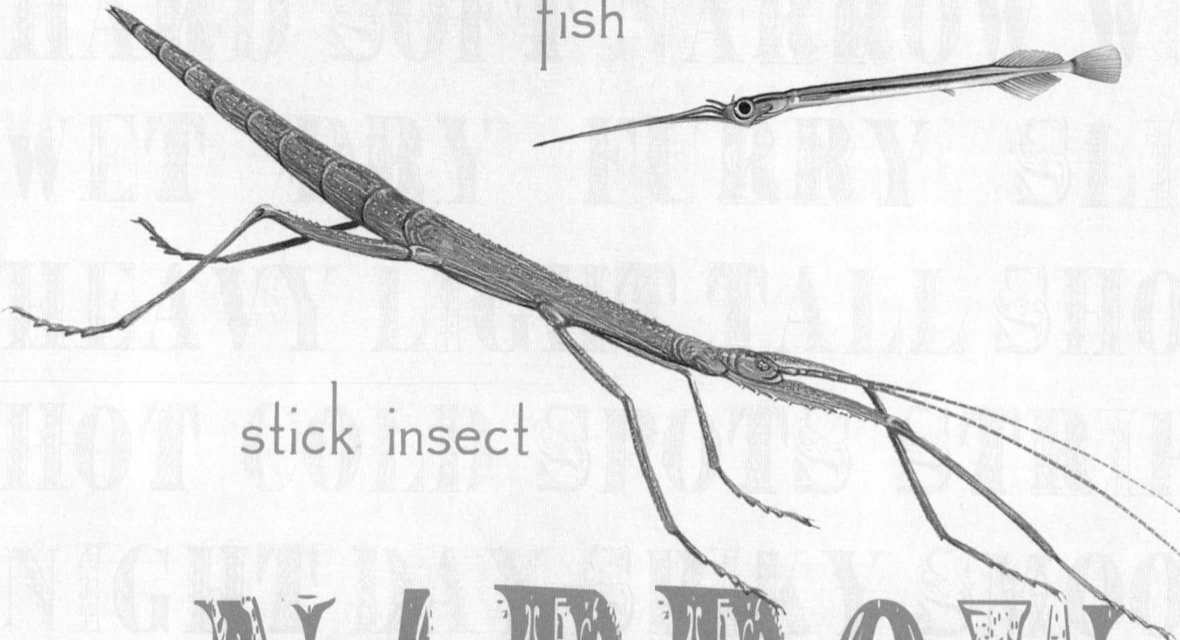

stick insect

NARROW

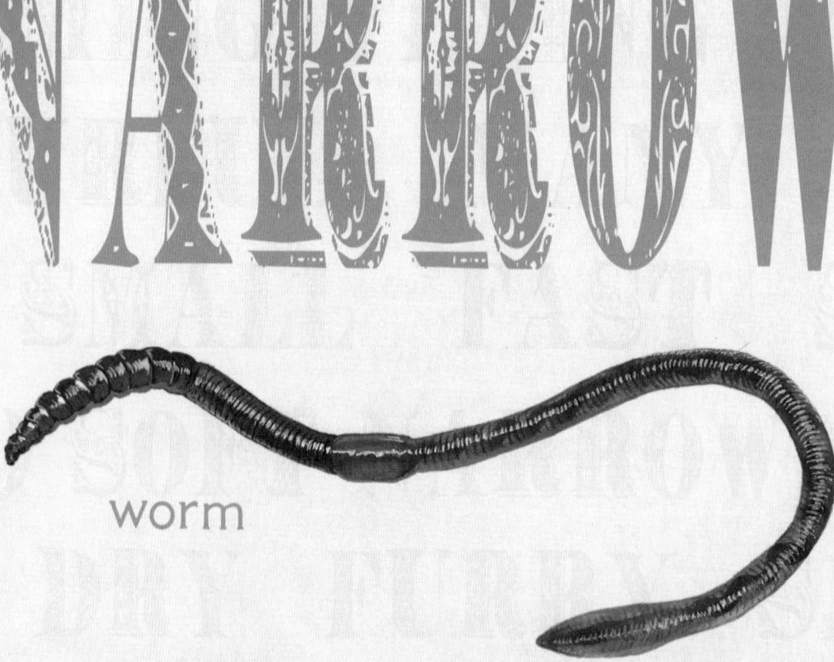

worm

W I D E

hippopotamus

ray

WET

seal

shark

tuna

fox

lizard

DRY

gerbil

kowari

hyena

FURRY

rabbit

panda

slug

SLIMY

frog

elephant

HEAVY

spider

moth

LIGHT

ant

jerboa

FEW
MANY
COLOURFUL
PLAIN
FLYING
SWIMMING
SMOOTH
SPIKY

camel

scorpion

rattlesnake

HOT

skink

penguin

COLD

polar bear

TALL giraffe

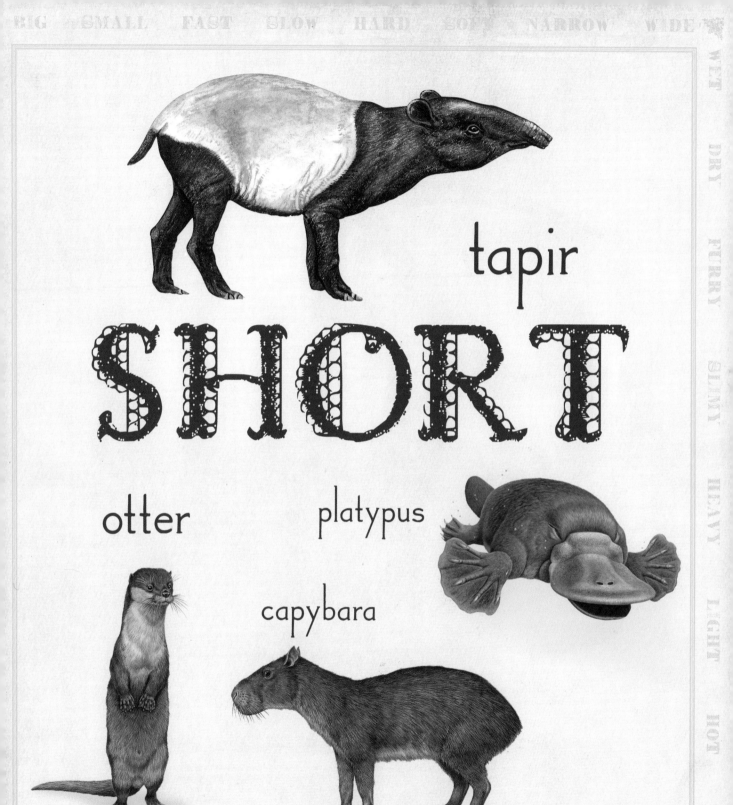

tapir

SHORT

otter   platypus

capybara

SPOTS

lizards

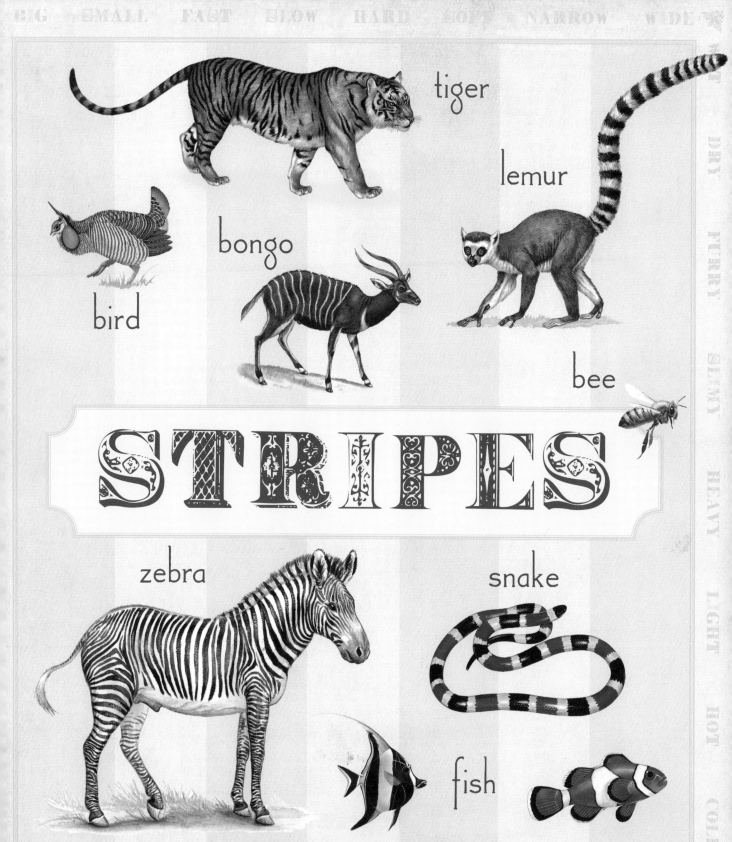

tiger

lemur

bongo

bird

bee

STRIPES

zebra

snake

fish

DAY

iguana

crocodile

bird

bee

SPIKY

sea urchin

porcupine

echidna

WET

DRY

FURRY

SLIMY

HEAVY

LIGHT

HOT

COLD

caecilian

SMOOTH

salamander

eel

dolphin

whale

seal

SWIMMING

fish

dragonfly

butterflies

FLYING

moth

bird

fly

rat

PLAIN

manatee

rhino

dipper

COLOURFUL

fish

bird

toad

Gila monster

MANY

fish

bear

FEW

This edition published in 2014
First published in 2013
Copyright © Marshall Editions 2013

All rights reserved. No part of this publication may be reproduced, stored in
a retrieval system, or transmitted in any form or by any means, electronic, mechanical,
photocopying, recording, or otherwise, without the prior permission of the publisher, nor be
otherwise circulated in any form of binding or cover other than that in whichit is published and
without a similar condition being imposed on the subsequent purchaser.

QED Publishing, a Quarto Group company
The Old Brewery
6 Blundell Street
London N7 9BH

www.qed_publishing.co.uk

A catalogue record for this book is available from the British Library.

ISBN 978 1 78171 685 4

Printed and bound in China by
1010 Printing International Ltd